Teechers

A Classroom Comedy

John Godber

Herefordshire Libraries
Readers Group Set
COPY
15

A SAMUEL FRENCH ACTING EDITION

SAMUEL FRENCH

FOUNDED 1830

SAMUELFRENCH.COM
SAMUELFRENCH-LONDON.CO.UK

FOR PRODUCTION ENQUIRIES

UNITED STATES AND CANADA
Info@SamuelFrench.com
1-866-598-8449

UNITED KINGDOM AND EUROPE
Theatre@SamuelFrench-London.co.uk
020-7255-4302

Each title is subject to availability from Samuel French, depending upon country of performance. Please be aware that *TEECHERS* may not be licensed by Samuel French in your territory. Professional and amateur producers should contact the nearest Samuel French office or licensing partner to verify availability.

TEECHERS

First performed by the Hull Truck Theatre Company at the Edinburgh Festival, 1987, with the following cast of characters:

Salty (playing **Teacher B, Nixon, Pete Saxon, Oggy Moxon, Mr Fisher, Mr Hatton, Deanie**)	Martin Barass
Gail (playing **Teacher A, Ms Whitham, Oggy Moxon, Mr Basford, Miss Prime, Barry Wobschall, Dennis, Dough, Mrs Coates**)	Gill Tompkins
Hobby (playing **Mrs Parry, Ms Jones, Mr Basford, Ron, Piggy Patterson, Oggy Moxon, Mrs Clifton**)	Shirley Anne Selby

Directed by John Godber

The action takes place in a comprehensive school hall

Time—the present

AUTHOR'S NOTE

Teechers was designed to be played by three actors, multi-role playing twenty other parts in a play-within-a-play format. Everything about the production was reduced to the basic essentials: actors, stage, audience. I wanted to produce a play that relied on the same bare essentials that a drama teacher might have in school: kids (actors), a few chairs and desks (the set), and an audience. With these basic ingredients anything can happen in a drama lesson; indeed the characters in *Teechers* illustrate that once talent has been tapped in school the result is often staggering. Multi-role playing is also, it must be said, an economic as well as artistic consideration. Maybe if I had twenty actors at my disposal I would have produced a different play? In this version of the play the twenty multi-roled parts have been listed in order that twenty actors (kids) could perform the play if so desired. However the play is performed, actors or students, it is important to remember that *Teechers* is a comedy, a comedy which illustrates many anxieties in education today. Comedies must primarily be funny, here is a comedy, I think, which is also deadly serious.

The set

Nothing is required in the way of a set except for three plastic briefcases, old newspapers for the staff-room scenes, a broom for Doug, and two chairs and two open-top desks for the various other settings, all of which should be easily obtained in school. When produced by three actors, character differentiation is helped by the use of funny noses (which the kids would have bought cheaply from W. H. Smith's). Clearly when the play is produced with a larger cast a proportional increase in props is to be expected.

The music

Any incidental music in the play should be contemporary chart music.

CHARACTERS

Salty—A school-leaver, bright and fresh-faced, rather dirty in appearance

Gail—Loud-mouthed and bossy, attractive and full of enthusiasm

Hobby—Shy. Should be very large, must be bigger than the other two. She is doing the play despite herself

Nixon—New drama teacher, young and casual

Mrs Parry—The Head Mistress, large and loud, a real eccentric

Mr Basford—The Deputy Head, a typical child hater, a nasty piece of work

Miss Prime—Dolly bird of a PE mistress

Ms Whitham—A fussy and hopeless teacher, deperate to leave

Ms Jones—A moaner, rather fat, someone who wants to leave but no-one will employ her

Deanie—A teacher who thinks all the kids love him, a bad dancer

Doug—The caretaker, a miserable old man, he hates kids and drama

Oggy—The cock of the school, looks much older than he actually is, the school bully in a modern age

Pete Saxon—A large, frightening youth with tattoos, appears foolish

Mr Fisher—Head of PE

Barry Wobschall—A small boy who never brings his PE kit

Piggy Patterson—A boy who is always telling on others, he always runs to his lessons

Ron—A boy who never does PE

Mr Hatton—Helps with the youth club dance

Dennis—Oggy's side-kick

Mrs Coates—Head Mistress at Saint George's

Mrs Clifton—Head of Governors at Saint George's

ACT I

A comprehensive school hall

A wooden stage. There are two double desks US. UR *is an old locker with a school broom leaning against it.* DC *is a chair;* L *and* R *two single desks and chairs angled* DS, *and three bags. A satchel, plastic bags and sports bags are near the chairs and desks. They belong to Salty, Gail and Hobby respectively*

Some music plays and Salty, Gail and Hobby enter, recline on the chairs and desks and look at the audience for a moment before speaking

Salty No more school for us so you can knackers!
Gail Salty, you nutter?
Salty What?
Gail Swearing.
Hobby Shurrup.
Salty So what?
Hobby You daft gett.
Salty It's true.
Gail Just get on with it.
Salty Nobody can do us.
Hobby We've not left yet.
Salty Knackers.
Gail Oh God he's craacked.
Hobby Shurrup.
Salty I've always wanted to be on this stage. I've always wanted to come up here and say, "knackers". I bet you all have. Whenever I see Mrs Hudson come up on this stage to talk about litter or being a good samaritan or corn dollies or sit down first year stand up second year I think about that word. 'Cos really Mrs Hudson would like to come up here and say, "knackers school". She would.
Gail Are we doing this play or what?
Salty It's like when she gets you in her office, all neat and smelling of perfume and she says, "You don't come to school to fool around, Ian, to waste your time. We treat you like young adults and we expect you to behave accordingly. I don't think that writing on a wall is a mature thing to do."
Hobby That's good that, Salty, just like her.
Salty Yeh, but really she wants to say, "Hey, Salty, pack all this graffiti in, it's getting on my knackers."
Gail Are we starting?
Salty Anyway why am I bothered. No more school, no more stick, no more teachers thinking that you're thick . . .

Gail No more of Miss Jubb shouting like you're deaf as a post, "Gail Saunders how dare you belch in front of me." Sorry, miss, didn't know it was your turn ...

Hobby Brilliant ...

Salty Hey, no more full school assemblies sat on the cold floor of the sports hall freezing your knackers off ...

Hobby No more cross-country running, and cold showers and towels that don't dry you.

Gail Oh and no more scenes in changing rooms where you daren't get changed because you wear a vest and everyone has got a bra ...

Hobby No more Mr Thorn sending letters home about how I missed games and was seen eating a kebab in the *Golden Spoon*.

Gail No more sweaty geog teachers with Brylcream hush puppies.

Salty No more trendy art teachers, who say "Hiya" and "Call me Gordon" ...

Hobby We haven't had an art teacher called Gordon.

Salty I know.

Gail No more having to run the fifteen hundred metres with a heart condition.

Salty No more.

Hobby 'Cos today we're off. Twagging it for ever.

Gail Let's start Salty.

Salty Hang on, before we do start, we all want to thank Mr Harrison, our new drama teacher. Before he came to this school, last September, us three didn't do sod all, not a thing. He got us into this, he's a good bloke. You are, sir. I know that he's been offered a job at a better school ... Well good luck to him ... Before Mr Harrison came here, the teachers had given us up for dead ... We were average.

Hobby Lillian is average, she opens her book well, and likes a warm room.

Gail Gail is stagnant to inert, and fights when cornered. Average.

Salty I don't feel average today, I feel top of the class ... thanks to sir.

Hobby I never thought I'd be doing this, I hated drama, only took it for a doss about ...

Salty Right, don't forget to keep in character, and Hobby, always face the front.

Hobby I will do.

Gail And speak up.

Hobby I will do.

Salty A lot of the stuff in the play was told to us by Mr Harrison ...

Gail And even though you might not believe it, everything what happens in the play is based on truth.

Hobby But the names and the faces have been changed.

Salty To protect the innocent.

Gail We're going to take you to Whitewall High School. It's a comprehensive school somewhere in England ... And they're expecting a new teacher to arrive.

Hobby There's fifteen hundred kids at Whitewall and it's a Special Priority Area which means that it's got its fair share of problems ...

Salty All we want you to do is use your imagination because there's only three of us, and we all have to play different characters ...
Hobby And narrators ...
Salty And narrators.
Hobby So you'll have to concentrate ...
Salty Oh yeh, you'll have to concentrate ...
Gail Title ...
Salty Oh shit, yeh ... And it's called *Teechers*.

A sudden burst of music. They become teachers, with briefcases and files, walking about a number of corridors. The Lights become brighter

Salty Morning.
Gail Morning.
Hobby Morning.
Salty Morning.
Hobby Morning.
Gail Morning.
Parry Stop running Simon Patterson.
Teacher A Morning, Ted.
Parry Morning, Roy.
Teacher B Morning, Mr Basford.
All Morning, Mrs Parry ...
Parry Good-morning ...
Witham You are chewing, girl, spit it out. Not into her hair, into a bin ...
Teacher B I don't call that a straight line, do you, Claire Dickinson? No? Neither do I.
Parry I know that was the bell, Simon Patterson. The bell is a signal for me to move and not for anyone else.

Music

Nixon I'm Jeff Nixon the new drama teacher. I'm looking for Mrs Parry's office.
Hobby Up the steps in the nice part of the school, first left.

Salty exits

Gail }
Hobby } *(together)* Mmmmmmmmmmm.
Gail He doesn't look much like a teacher, he looks like somebody who's come to mend the drains.

Salty enters as Nixon

Nixon I knew at my interview that Whitewall had a bad reputation and no drama facilities. But like a sheriff with my brand-new degree pinned to my chest I bounded up to Mrs Parry's office ... She was busy ... With Mr Basford the Deputy Head.

Gail dons a facial mask, nose and glasses, which all the cast wear as Mr Basford

Basford I don't believe you're doing this.

Parry I run it and I shall do what I like.

Basford After all the work I've put in, now you turn around and tell me that I'm not Koko ... Great. It's a bloody liberty.

Parry Mr Basford, I'm sorry ... But there is nothing else to say ... I need a younger person. I'm sure you'll have a great deal of fun in the chorus.

Basford In the chorus. I wouldn't be seen dead in the chorus.

Parry It's that or nothing, good-day, I have another appointment. Mrs Parry, or should I say Cordelia Parry, BA M.Ed. was a huge attractive woman. She carried herself very well but had awful dress sense, and would often mix pink with yellow. She was of large frame with a voice to match. Mr Nixon? Jeff Nixon?

Nixon That's right.

Parry Hello, nice to see you again. Coffee?

Nixon Please. Mrs Parry's office was a cavern of theatre posters ... She certainly had more than a passing interest.

Parry Drama! Bare boards and a passion. Wonderful. This is my all-male production of *The Trojan Women*, and this is me as Ophelia.

Nixon Behind her head was a photo of a much lither Mrs Parry in an amateur production of *Hamlet*.

Parry I'm doing *The Mikado* in the spring term, Mr Nixon.

Nixon I knew exactly what she meant.

Parry I'm looking for a Koko ...

Nixon It must be difficult.

Parry Mr Basford usually takes the leads in our local G and S productions but I'm afraid he was rather tiresome last year in *The Pirates* ... We're looking for new blood ... Well that's given you something to think about, hasn't it?

Nixon It certainly has.

Parry And so to business, Mr Nixon.

Nixon The meeting went on for another twenty minutes, but I got the message. Keep any eye off for the teacher-eating girls and the thuggish boys ... they'll have you for breakfast.

Gail But one thing struck him about Mrs Parry. She really did care about the kids at Whitewall.

Parry As we walked from my office, that is Mrs Parry's ... I wished Jeff all the luck with his probationary year, and took him towards Mr Basford's room, home of the timetable. Here we are.

Nixon The gigantic timetable was screwed to the wall. It was so colourful, so meticulous, it was a work of art, like something from the Vatican. A life's work had gone into making it.

Parry The nomenclature is fairly straightforward. You will be N.I., Mr Nixon, and drama will be D.R. As you'll be having your lessons in the Main Hall, drama with you in the Main Hall, would read N.I.D.R.M.H. If you have a first-year class it could read, N.I.D.R. M.H.I.Y.X. Period one. Fairly simple.

Nixon Elementary, Mrs Parry.

Parry If you have any problems at all, Jeff, don't hesitate, come up and see me straight away, I'm always available. And don't forget about *The Mikado*. I know how much the theatre must be in your blood . . . It could be your big break . . .

Nixon So I tentatively said "yes", to a small part in the chorus, and although Mrs Parry was disappointed that I didn't want Koko, she said that I would certainly enjoy my time in Titipu.

A corridor

Gail Excuse me, sir?
Nixon Eh?
Gail Sir, I'm lost.
Nixon Well where should you be?
Gail Sir, I don't know, I can't work it out on my timetable. I'm in tutor group I.D. But I'm in teaching group I.Y.Five and I should be in block Four.Three.B doing biology. But Three.Y.Y.Six are in there with Mr Dean doing history, he says that I should be in Three.One.D. but I've been there and the class is empty. Sir, I've been looking for my class for forty minutes.
Nixon What have you got next?
Gail PE in the gym.
Nixon Do you know where that is?
Gail Yes, sir.
Nixon Well I suggest that you go and wait there, then at least your class'll find you.
Gail Right, thanks sir . . .
Nixon Oh, before you go. Have you any idea where Nine.I.B. is?

A pause. We are now in the Form Room

Hobby When you're a hardnut and fifteen you always have to give teachers a bad time. It's part of the rules of the game . . . And when there's a new teacher you can be even tougher. In our class we had seen off three tutors in as many weeks.
Gail Miss Bell had a breakdown, but said she was pregnant.
Hobby Then we had a supply teacher who was always crying . . .
Gail And then they sent old Mr Willcox who was deaf so that was a laugh, we used to say anything to him.
Hobby And now they've sent us a new teacher. A brand-new, sparkling clean, not even out of the box teacher . . .
Teacher A They're only going to be in school for two more terms . . . Send them the new bloke Nixon . . . He can cut his teeth on Seven.Y.Y. down in Nine.I.B. . . . It's out of the way – if they eat him or burn him alive we can forget about him.
Salty In Seven.Y.Y. there was me, Salty, Gail and Hobby who you know, Kevin Mears – who spoke funny . . . All right, Kevin?
Gail Not bad, Salty, all right . . . I've been down to our Malcolm's, he's got a brilliant BMX. We had a great game of rally cross.
Salty Kev was fifteen going on three. There was John Frogett who never wore any decent shoes.

Gail Sally Wrenshaw . . .
Hobby Vicky Marshall.
Salty Walter Jones.
Gail Fancy calling a kid Walter . . .
Salty And Trisha Foreshore who had been through nearly all the kids in the school . . . except me.
Gail Salty, that's not true . . .
Salty It is.
Gail It is not.
Salty Right you ask Benny Good.
Gail I wouldn't ask Benny Good what the time was . . . He's a big mouth and a liar . . .
Hobby Oh come on get on with it . . .
Salty And Trisha Foreshore who was known, but it might not be true, as being a bit of a goer.
Gail That's better . . .
Hobby When they sent you a new teacher, it was like getting some foster parents . . . When Nixon arrived we were bored and disinterested.
Nixon Hi . . . Is this Nine.I.B . . . ? I'm Mr Nixon . . . It's a bit chilly in here isn't it? Can you two lads come down from the bookshelves, I don't think that they were meant for sitting on, were they? If you don't mind—just come down. And if you could stop playing table tennis that would also help. Can everybody sit on a seat and not on a desk? That's better . . . Right . . . My name is Mr Nixon.

Gail and Hobby laugh

The entire class burst into laughter. I didn't see that I'd said anything funny. My name is fairly straightforward and I've only got one head. I turned to the blackboard and saw that some joker had drawn some enormous genitals on the board. I looked at the class, they were still laughing. "Bollocks" is not spelt with an "x" . . .
Hobby I don't like him.
Gail You've got to give him a chance.
Hobby Why, do you like him?
Gail No but . . . We even gave Miss Bell a chance.
Hobby He's trying to be too smart . . . I hate teachers who call you by your nickname.
Gail Yeh, but you hate being called Lillian. Everybody calls you Hobby.
Hobby So what, that's no reason why he should, he's new.

A school bell rings. Each actor goes to a desk, as kids. They address the audience as staff

A number of classrooms

Whitham Right quieten down, quieten down, said Maureen Whitham, scale two humanities, as she pathetically tried to control a class of thirty. Please be quiet. If you don't keep quiet I'll have to get Mr Basford . . . Be quiet . . . Shut up . . . Hush . . . Shhh!

Nixon As I walked through the maze of a school I heard and saw many different types of teaching.

Whitham Please, don't throw the books about, it's one between three, now everyone be quiet . . . BE QUIET.

Nixon It was like a menagerie.

Hobby becomes Mr Basford

Basford Nobody speaks in Mr Basford's lessons. That's why I have the best maths results in the school. Nobody talks, you can't work and talk, nobody can not even me, and I'm a genius . . .

Nixon Most classes had some sort of noise coming from them . . .

Whitham Right, said Maureen Whitham, as she hopelessly tried to settle her class . . . I'm going to get Mr Basford . . . Oh . . . Silence, that's better . . .

Nixon Mr Basford's class, worked in absolute silence, with absolute commitment. He also had the best kids.

Basford Don't let the bastards grind you down, hit 'em low and hard . . . low and hard, kids respect discipline . . . If they don't get it at home, they get it in my lessons . . . Hush down . . . I can hear someone breathing . . .

The Main Hall

Nixon I arrived at my first lesson five minutes late, I'd taken a wrong turn at block one and found myself in the physics block . . . A fifth year non-exam drama group lounged about some stacked chairs in the main hall . . . Sixteen of them had managed to turn up. Twenty-five names were on the register. The school hall looked like a youth club; I walked purposefully to the stage.

Gail Oh God it's him, Dixon.

Hobby Got him for tutor and for drama.

Gail What's happened to Mrs Hugill?

Hobby Left. I hate drama. Only did it for a skive.

Gail Yeh and me, it was this or music. Got any cigs?

Hobby They wouldn't let me do music, said I was too clumsy. I've got two Woodbines, my granny's.

Gail Buy a tab off you at break?

Nixon Get a chair, I said in a friendly, sort of youth worker type of tone.

Hobby What's he say?

Nixon Grab a chair everyone . . .

Gail We're not doing any work, are we, sir?

Nixon Can you grab a chair . . .

Gail I'll give you some crisps if I can tab you . . .

Nixon Can you all please get a chair and come and sit around the stage in a half-circle . . .

Hobby How long have you been smoking?

Gail About four months . . .

Hobby Why don't you buy some bastard cigs then . . .

Gail I am going to do.

Hobby When?

Gail Tomorrow ...

Nixon Can you get a chair and stop waving them around? I know I just said get a chair but I didn't expect you to swing it around your head ...

Hobby If I tab you and you don't bring any cigs I'll drop you ...

Gail I will, honest ... Honest, I will ...

Nixon Get a chair and sit on the BASTARD ...

Gail What's he say?

Hobby Dunno.

Nixon Will everyone please sit on a chair?

Gail Who's he think he is?

Hobby Are you going to bio or are you twagging it?

Gail Is she here?

Hobby Her car's here. It's that red 'un.

Gail I'm off downtown then, get a milk shake.

Nixon When everyone is ready ... Good ... I think it would be a good thing for us to start with a very important person in the world of drama. Mr William Shakespeare. And in particular a play that you've probably seen but don't realize it. *Romeo and Juliet*.

Gail and Hobby groan

Which is a tragedy.

Gail And it's the basis for *West Side Story*, and it's about neighbours arguing.

Hobby We've done it ...

Nixon Oh ...

Hobby We did it with Mrs Hugill.

Gail And we did about two tramps who're waiting for somebody and he never turns up.

Hobby And that was boring.

Gail And we've done *Hamlet*. About a prince who kills his uncle. Haven't we?

Hobby Yeh. And two killers who are after somebody and one of 'em's a deaf and dumb waiter.

Gail And we've done *Beverly Hills Cop. Beverly Hills Cop Two* ...

Hobby *Neighbours* ...

Gail *Eastenders* ... "Hello, Arfur ... All right, my love."

Hobby Good that ...

Gail What else have we done?

Hobby *Indiana Jones*.

Gail Yeh. *Jewel of the Nile* ... We've done all there is in drama ...

Nixon At that moment, a giant of a lad, Peter Saxon stood up. He must have been six feet seven, with tatoos on his arms and a line across his neck which read, "Cut here." "I wanna say something", he said, "I've got some drama to tell you ..." "Go on then, Peter", I said; not knowing what to expect ... (*He becomes Pete Saxon*) Right I'm Peter Saxon now ... One day, sir, last year, it was great. Me and Daz Horne decided to run away, to seek our fortune. We was going to go to London. It was a Tuesday, I think. But it could have been a Thursday. No, no, it was a Tuesday, 'cos we had Mr Cooper for technical drawing. Mr Cooper's soft, sir, you can swear at him and all sorts, we used to call him "gibbon head", 'cos he had a bald head and looked like a gibbon. Anyway, me and Daz are in his class and I throws a chair at him, so he goes and hides himself in a storeroom, so me and Horney lock him in the storeroom, and then we get a chair and stand on it and look at him through the window in the top of the storeroom, and I keeps shouting "gibbon head" to him . . . Anyway, then we twags it and gets a bus to the station. I couldn't stop laughing, sir, honest, just the picture of gibbon head sat in that storeroom killed me off. Anyway, Horney says that we've got drama with Mrs Hugill before dinner, so we comes back to do our drama lesson. In drama we did "different visions of hell". I was a cyclops and Horney was my mam. Anyway, me and Horney got into stacks of trouble. But I liked doing plays when Mrs Hugill was here . . . Sir, as far as I know sir, Mr Cooper is still locked in the storeroom . . .

Gail He's a liar . . .

Nixon That was good, Peter. The kids had raw potential, but I had to get them into plays. They were a funny bunch, but I think they liked me, and I liked them. Whitewall wasn't so bad.

Gail Sir? Can we do *E.T.*?

Hobby }
Gail } (*together*) E.T., phone home . . .

Music

The Staff-room

Nixon After the first month I was beginning to feel fairly confident. And I also had my eye on Jackie Prime, PE mistress.

Prime Jackie Prime was tall, sun-tanned, bouncy and an expert at net ball and tennis . . . She was developing dance in the gym and took an interest in all games.

Nixon Morning.

Prime Morning.

Nixon How did the first eleven get on?

Prime Lost sixty-seven nil. Saint George's team are in a different class . . . and Oggy Moxon, our captain, was sent off for spitting.

Nixon Who's Oggy Moxon?

Prime He's the best player we've got. But he's a handful.

Nixon I see.

Prime Have you tasted the coffee? It's like something brought back from a field trip.

Nixon It was eight pence and was forced down you by Madge the tea-lady.

Prime We have our own kettle in the gym. For PE staff only.

Parry Morning.

Teacher A }
Teacher B } (*together*) Morning, Mrs Parry.

Parry Morning, Mr Nixon. I hope you're still thinking about *The Mikado*. I wouldn't want your mind to wander on to other things.

Nixon Don't worry, Mrs Parry, I'll be at rehearsals.

Parry Good, Mr Nixon. Good. Did you know Whitewall has a farm?

Prime Well it's not actually a farm Mrs Parry, we do have a pig.

Parry My dear Miss Prime, we have a number of pigs.

Prime One's an old sow.

Nixon And geese?

Parry Two geese.

Nixon I was doing duty around the back of the canteen, I was attacked by the geese . . . But I have discovered how to avoid the smokers, simply look the other way . . .

Prime Look I must go, I've got baths. It's fairly obvious where the kids are going to smoke, and if you want to catch the smokers you can, but if I was you, I wouldn't go behind the Sports Hall . . .

Nixon Why?

Prime That's Oggy Moxon's patch. All the staff leave Oggy well alone.

Nixon And then she left. She was a breath of fresh air . . . A bubble in an otherwise flat brew . . . Oh God . . . I was becoming infatuated with Jackie Prime.

Gail But Jackie Prime didn't see Nixon as anything at all. When she looked, he wasn't there, he was just another teacher and she was being sociable.

Jones You can't sit there, that's Marcus' seat.

Nixon What about over here?

Jones That's someone's seat. Frank Collier's.

Nixon Oh, right. Is this anyone's paper?

Whitham Yes. It's Deany's, he's on the loo . . .

Nixon I can't share a cheek on the edge of that, can I, Mavis?

Jones Sorry, Jeff . . .

Nixon Even after seven weeks finding a regular seat in the staff-room was a nightmare. I was told by Mr Dean that a lot of new staff preferred to stand outside in the rain. Mr Sawyer had been at Whitewall's for two years and not ever got a seat in the staff-room.

Whitham I do not believe he is doing this. Look at the timetable, Basford's gone bananas.

Nixon I longed to be down in the gym and have a cup of tea with Jackie Prime. But—it was a forlorn fantasy.

Whitham The man does not care, he just doesn't care.

Jones What's the matter, Maureen?

Whitham I'm on cover for Mick Edward's remedial English group. I hate them. I do. I hate that group . . .

Jones I know what you mean . . . I've just had Trisha Foreshore, if that girl says "I'm bored, miss" once again I'll ring her soddin' neck.

Whitham But they hate me, he knows they do. It's not fair . . .

Jones Do you know what she says . . . We're looking at the digestive system, and she says "Miss, the oesophagus is one long tube running from mouth to anus". I said "Very good, Trisha, how did you find that out?" She says "Miss, I went to the dentist and he looked in my mouth and he could tell that I'd got diarrhoea". I said "It's pyorrhoea, girl, pyorrhoea, bleeding gums . . ." I give up on some of 'em, I really do . . .

Whitham Remedial English. He knows I've got a doctorate and he puts me on remedial English.

Nixon There was another big fight at break-time. Silly sods.

Music

Back of the Sports Hall

Gail The cock of Whitewall High was Bobby Moxon, known to all and sundry as——

Salty —Oggy Moxon.

Gail There was no doubt at all that Oggy was dangerous, all the teachers gave him a wide berth. He was sixteen going on twenty-five, rumour had it that he had lost his virginity when he was ten and that Miss Prime fancied the pants off him.

Hobby When Oggy Moxon said "shit", you did, when he said it was Wednesday, it was Wednesday.

Gail One Wednesday, I was stood outside one of the mobile classrooms, Mr Dean had sent me out of the class. I'd told him that I thought Peter the Great was a bossy gett!! And he sent me out . . . I'm stood there with a mood on when Oggy comes past.

Salty becomes Oggy Moxon

Oggy All right, Gail?

Gail Yeh. I knew that he fancied me.

Oggy What you doing?

Gail Waiting for Christmas, what's it look like?

Oggy I'm having a party in my dad's pub, wanna come? Most of the third year is coming . . . Should be a good night . . .

Gail Might come then.

Oggy Might see you there.

Gail Might.

Oggy Wear something that's easy to get off. Your luck might be in.

Gail I hate him.

Hobby I do.

Gail Somebody ought to drop him.

Hobby Who? All the staff shit themselves when they have to teach him.

Gail Oggy Moxon's speech about being hard: I'm Oggy Moxon . . . We said you'd have to use your imaginations . . . I'm Oggy, I'm as hard as nails, as toe-capped boots I'm hard, as marble in a church, as concrete on your head I'm hard. As calculus I'm hard. As learning Hebrew is hard, then so am I. Even Basford knows I'm rock, his cane wilts like an old sock . . . And if any teachers in the shitpot school with their degrees and bad breath lay a finger on me, God be my judge, I'll have their hides . . . And if not me, our Nobby will be up to this knowledge college in a flash . . . All the female flesh fancy me in my "five-o-ones", no uniform for me never. From big Mrs Grimes to pert Miss Prime I see their eyes flick to my button-holed flies. And they know like I that no male on this staff could satisfy them like me, 'cos I'm hard all the time. Last Christmas dance me

and Miss Prime pranced to some bullshit track and my hand slipped
down her back, and she told me she thought that I was great, I felt that
arse, that schoolboy wank, a tight-buttocked, Reebok-footed, leggy-arse
... I touched that and heard her sigh ... for me. And as I walk my last
two terms through these corridors of sickly books and boredom ... I see
grown men flinch and fear ... In cookery one day my hands were all
covered with sticky paste, and in haste I asked pretty Miss Bell if she
could get for me a hanky from my pockets, of course she would, a student
on teaching practice – wanting to help, not knowing my pockets had
holes and my underpants were in the wash ... "Oh no", she yelped, but in
truth got herself a thrill, and has talked of nothing else these last two years
... Be warned, when Oggy Moxon is around get out your cigs ... And
lock up your daughters ...

*Music plays. Gail and Hobby pick up a chair each; they are about to put the
chairs on the desks at the end of a lesson. Nixon puts on his coat. They
buttonhole him, they want to talk to him. He hangs around, really wanting to
be elsewhere*

Gail Sir, are teachers rich?
Nixon (*as if in anguish*) Noooo!
Gail What about Mrs Parry, she's got a massive car?
Nixon She might be, but I'm not.
Hobby Are you married, sir?
Nixon (*another difficult response*) No. Next question.

*Hobby and Gail try and think of another question which will have the effect of
keeping Nixon talking to them. Meanwhile he picks up his briefcase*

Gail Sir, is this a school for thickies?
Nixon Why?
Gail 'Cos when we're going home, all the kids from the posh school, Saint
George's ... ask us if we can add up, and they ask us if we've got any table
tennis homework?
Hobby Sir, all the kids who go to that school are snobs ... Their dads drive
big cars ...
Gail And they call us "divvies" ...
Hobby Sir, because they go there they think they're better than us.
Gail And, they say our teachers are shit. Oh sorry, didn't mean to say that.
Hobby Mr Basford's sons go there, don't they?
Gail Yeh, two twins. "Twinnies" they're called. They're right brainy ... Sir,
have you got a girlfriend?
Nixon Not at the moment.
Gail Brilliant.
Hobby Do you like it at this school, sir?
Nixon Yeh, it's OK, you lot are awkward, but OK.
Hobby Sir, what do you think it's most important for a teacher to do?
Nixon Well, I think a teacher should have a good relationship, if he hasn't
got a relationship he can only ever be a teacher, never a person.

Gail What about Mr Basford, he hasn't got a good relationship with the kids . . .

Nixon Well I can't speak for Mr Basford, can I?

Hobby Sir, the bell's gone . . .

Nixon You'd better go and get it then—and go quietly. (*A pause*) It was a trip to see *The Rocky Horror Show* that got me really close to those three, although I had to watch my step with Gail, she kept putting her hand on my leg during the sexy bits . . .

Hobby Science fiction . . . Whooooo. Double Feature.

Gail Doctor X has built a creature.

Hobby becomes Mr Basford

Nixon Mr Basford you wanted to see me?

Basford Mr Nixon, I understand you took a group of fifteen-year olds to see a play featuring transvestites from Transylvania? I can imagine what educational value that has.

Nixon A black mark from Basford. Mrs Parry had omitted to tell me about the joys of doing cover . . . Usually a student would appear like the ghost of Caesar and present you with a pink slip, this would tell you where to go and who to cover for. Mr Basford was in charge of the cover rota.

Basford Nixon N.I. to cover for Fisher F.I. third year games . . . And the best of luck.

The Gymnasium

Prime All right, all third year deadlegs from Mr Fisher's group shut up, said Miss Jackie Prime. If you want to watch the nineteen seventy-four World Cup Final on video go to the lecture theatre with Mr Clarke's group. Those who want to play pirates in the gym get changed, you without kit better see Mr Nixon.

Hobby A whole line of kids wearing anoraks came forward . . . Mr Nixon looked staggered, he'd been left to deal with PE's cast offs.

Gail And amongst the throng was the legendary Barry Wobschall. Barry never did sport. He hated games.

Hobby Barry was fifteen but had the manner of an old man, he lived with his grandad and spoke with all the wisdom of someone four times his age. Every day for the past two years he had worked on a milk round.

Nixon Where's your kit?

Ron Sir, my shorts don't fit me.

Nixon What about you?

Piggy Sir, my mother put my shorts in the wash and they got chewed up because the washer has gone all wrong . . .

Nixon Oh yeh.

Piggy It's true, sir, honest.

Nixon What about you, Barry Wobschall, have you got any kit?

Barry No, sir.

Piggy He never brings any kit, sir.

Nixon I wasn't asking you, was I, Simon Patterson.

Piggy No, sir.

Nixon What about a note, Barry? Have you brought a note?
Barry Sir.
Nixon Oh let's have it then.
Gail Barry handed him the note. It was small and crumpled. Barry looked in innocence as Nixon opened the piece of paper.

Gail hands Nixon a piece of paper

Nixon (*reading*) "Please leave four pints and a yoghurt this Saturday".
Barry It's the only note I could get, sir.
Nixon I tried to talk Barry Wobschall into changing his options. His sort of humour in a drama class would have been dynamite. But he wouldn't change, he said he preferred doing geog, because it was peaceful and he liked copying maps.
Gail On the thirteenth of October Jackie Prime was at the GCSE meeting held at Saint George's . . . She was walking around the quadrant. A choir was singing.

A choir sings

Nixon It's beautiful.
Prime There's been . . .
Nixon It's just a different world. I hear they're opting out.
Prime It's very likely. They've got a fantastic drama studio, dance facilities.
Nixon If they opt out they'll charge fees . . . It'll be like a private school.
Prime They say that they won't, but maybe they will. Only time will tell.
Nixon Mr Basford's kids come here.
Prime You sound surprised . . . And Jackie Prime was off, into Saint George's gymnasium.
Nixon It was fantastic. There was something reassuring about Saint George's that made you want to teach there. Something soothing and academic, the same, I was beginning to think, could not be said of Whitewall.

The choir stops

Back of the Sports Hall. Gail, as Dennis, and Hobby, as Oggy Moxon, are flicking through a magazine

Dennis Where did you get it?
Oggy My dad gets 'em delivered in brown paper parcels . . .
Dennis 'S have a look.
Oggy It's disgusting . . .
Dennis What is, what is?
Hobby Oggy had stolen one of his father's dirty magazines, for fifty pence third year's could have a quick look. For a quid first year's could have a glance.
Gail It was break and Oggy and Dennis are sharing a few cigs and a finger through Oggy's dad's magazine.
Nixon What're you doing, lads?
Oggy Nothing . . . I'm Oggy.

Nixon Well, you're obviously doing something.
Oggy No we're not.
Nixon You're not smoking, are you?
Dennis No.
Oggy What if we are?
Nixon It'll stunt your growth, you know?
Oggy So what?
Nixon What have you got there?
Oggy A book.
Nixon I know it's a book.
Oggy It's my dad's so if I was you I'd leave it with us.
Nixon Well I think that I'm going to have to report you.
Oggy Good. You do that.
Nixon You know what that means, don't you?
Oggy Yeh, I'll get kicked out of school with any luck. Great. I don't want to be here, anyway.
Gail By this time a massive crowd had gathered. Various voices shouted, "Smack him, Oggy. He's only a drama teacher."
Nixon I think you'd better come with me to see Mr Basford.
Oggy Big deal, he's not going to do anything.
Nixon Oh, really?
Oggy Yeh, really.
Nixon Well we'll see about that. I might have to deal with you myself.
Oggy What you gonna do, sir? Pretend I'm a tree?
Nixon I'm going to have to report you.
Oggy That's tough of you, why don't you have a go with me now, just me and you?
Nixon I'm going to have to report you.
Oggy You do that, sir . . .
Nixon And I turned and walked away, with kids jeering and shouting in the background. And very faintly I heard Oggy Moxon say . . .
Oggy You wanker . . .
Nixon It was my first horrific confrontation. I'd played it all wrong . . . I couldn't deal with Oggy. And if I couldn't, who I thought was fairly streetwise, what about Mrs Grimes, or Julie Sharpe or those nice quiet supply teachers who never have a wrong word for anyone?
Hobby As Nixon walked back to report Oggy, he started to think about getting out of teaching. He started to wish his probationary year away . . .
Nixon I wasn't talking to you. I was talking to Paul Drewitt, now will everyone hush down? I shan't say it again. All right, we'll wait till everyone's quiet before we go home.
Piggy Sir, the bell's gone.
Nixon I know the bell's gone, Simon Patterson, and I'm not bothered, I can stay here, all night!

Gail exits. Music

The Drama Club

During September I held "drama club" in the school hall after four
o'clock. Salty, Gail and Hobby were regulars, we did all sorts of work.
But it didn't really meet with the approval of Doug, the caretaker.

Nixon and Hobby play some scenes from "The Witches" in Macbeth

Gail, as Doug the caretaker, enters

Doug Come on let's have you, Niko, time to go home. I thought you lot
were withdrawing good will? Come on it's half-five let's have you. Time to
go find a space somewhere else.

Nixon Just five more minutes, Doug?

Doug No come on . . . I've got this floor to buffer. Mrs Parry's got a *Mikado*
rehearsal tonight for principals. And I've got the mobiles to do for night
class, and then the sports hall, 'cos five-a-side's on tonight. And somebody's gone crackers in the sixth form bogs . . .

Nixon Just give us a few more minutes, Doug . . .

Doug A few more minutes? Bloody hell, where would I be if I gave all the
staff a few more minutes?

Nixon Come on, Doug, don't be such an ogre.

Doug I'm asking you to leave, that's all.

Nixon But it's the manner of it . . .

Doug I've got to get this buffered that's all I'm bothered about . . .

Nixon It's taken me ages to get these interested in doing a play—do us a
favour, give me another twenty minutes . . .

Doug I can't, Mr Nixon . . . We're short-staffed . . . I've got three cleaners
off and Jim's back's playing him up . . . I'm only doing my job.

Nixon I'm only trying to do mine.

Doug Look, you don't get paid for this, get yourself off home . . .

Nixon I bet you wouldn't get Basford out of his office . . .

Doug You should have a proper room for this drama thing. I mean doing it
in the hall it's a disgrace . . . Sometimes I can't get a shine on the floor, I
have to polish it . . . And that's a bloody job.

Nixon If you can tell me, Doug, where there is any morsel of space for me to
do drama I'd be happy to move. Is there . . . Eh?

Doug Well, it's not worth bloody doing.

Nixon There isn't anywhere . . . I've got the Main Hall and that's it.

Doug If you ask me they should take it off, the bloody timetable, I mean,
they don't do any writing make as much noise as they bloody like, waste
of Education Authority's bloody money if you ask me.

Nixon You, silly old sod, you don't know what you're talking about.

Doug That's swearing, nobody swears at me, I don't get paid to be bloody
sworn at. Wait till I tell Mr Basford.

Doug moves to us. *Music*

The Staff-room

Nixon Thursday, November the ninth. Staff-room. One of my biggest fears
was that I was teaching the wrong book at O level. I had been doing
Twelfth Night for ten weeks when I heard a rumour on the grapevine that

the actual set book was *The Winter's Tale*. Mr Basford put me right on that, he also put me right on some other things.

Hobby becomes Mr Basford

Basford I hear that you've had a bit of a run-in with Doug. Don't upset the caretakers, Jeff, they do a great job.
Nixon I suppose we're all trapped in the same system. Kids. Staff. Caretakers. How are your lads doing at Saint George's?
Basford Fine.
Nixon You live out that way?
Basford Me? No. I live down Greenacre Parade.
Nixon That's this school's catchment area.
Basford That's right . . .
Nixon Why didn't they come to this school?
Basford (*after a pause*) St George's gets people into Oxford. Thirty per cent get five or more O levels that's why. Fifteen per cent get four here at Whitewall. Parents have the right to choose schools, and I'm choosing.
Nixon But St George's is ten miles away . . . It must cost a fortune . . .
Basford I'm making sure my kids have the best possible education.
Nixon And you can afford it. What about kids like Gail Saunders, can their parents pay for them to travel to St George's? No. They can't even afford to pay out for a school trip . . .
Basford So what am I supposed to do, make my lads disadvantaged because others are? Waken up, Jeff. Parents have a right to send kids to the school of their choice.
Nixon And kids have a right to a good education regardless of whether their parents have the ability or willingness to choose for them . . . You know as well as I do that a lot of parents don't attach a great deal of importance to education, that doesn't mean that we ditch their kids . . .
Basford Listen Mr Nixon . . . When you have any family, what will you want for your kids? Will you want them to do drama, let's say, in an old hall with no facilities and books that are sellotaped together or would you prefer they worked in an atmosphere where everything was new, and you could have what you wanted? You think about what you'd really want.
Nixon But that's not the point. Surely all schools should be the same, have the same facilities, have the same cash, cash made readily available. Shouldn't we want the best for all kids, not just those whose parents can pay to send them to a good school whether it be fees or bus fare? All kids deserve the right to be educated to their potential.
Basford And that's the sort of system we have now. A grade six kid is grade six potential.
Nixon That's bullshit and you know it. Examinations are a framework that we fit kids into.
Basford Do not talk to me like that, Mr Nixon.
Nixon And don't talk to me like that, you bloody fascist . . .
Basford I knew what you were as soon as I saw you.
Nixon What are you talking about?
Basford You know what I'm talking about, I'm talking about *The Mikado*.

Nixon What about it ... ?

Basford Eight years I've been in that society ...

Nixon And then he stormed off ...

Whitham "You've had it now," said Maureen Whitham, scale two Humanities, as she sat listening and thumbing through the *Times Ed*. Old Basford will make your life a misery, he'll have you on cover from now till eternity. Nobody calls Basford a fascist and gets away with it. The man's dangerous, I'd be careful tackling him. He's done a lot for the school. And after all they're his kids, he can do what he likes ...

Nixon I felt that I was wrong, that we shouldn't have a fair system, that we should let bright kids get bright and treat the less able kids like rhubarb, keep them in the dark and shit on 'em. And everywhere I looked I could see the difference between dog piss in Hobby's grandma's garden and garden parties and degrees at Saint George's. And the truth was that the garden party was what I wanted ... Whitewall was killing me, sapping me, frustrating me--wearing me down ... As Christmas approached I fell into a deep depression, I had two hundred first year reports to do, O level marking and the Christmas carol concerts meant that I couldn't get in the hall to teach.

Whitham Hey, Jeff, have you seen the *Times Ed*? Scale two going at Saint George's. Starts summer. A level theatre studies, drama studio ... Video equipment ...

Nixon No I'm not into that.

Whitham Oh you're not planning to stop here, are you? Everybody's trying to get out. They call this place "Colditz" at the County Hall. Don't be a mug, Jeff, when you see a hole in the fence go for it. I've got an interview coming up, in local radio ... Here, I'll leave it with you.

Hobby Mr Nixon?

Gail Sir?

Hobby Can I go to matron?

Nixon Look, come away from the gas taps.

Hobby Sir?

Nixon Just find a space.

Gail Sir, she's hit me.

Hobby Sir, I haven't.

Nixon Find a space.

Gail Sir, she has.

Hobby When will we be back in the hall?

Nixon Find a space!

Gail Are we doing the *Marat Sade*?

Hobby Can I go to matron?

Gail Are we doing *Billy Liar*?

Hobby Sir, she's taken my pen.

Gail Sir, I haven't.

Hobby Sir, she has, sir.

Gail Sir, I haven't.

Hobby Sir, she's taken my book.

Gail Sir, I haven't.
Hobby Sir, she's taken my partner.
Gail Sir, I haven't.
Hobby Sir, she's taken my glasses.
Gail Sir?
Hobby Mr Nixon.
Gail Sir?
Hobby Niko?
Gail Jeff?
Hobby Hey.
Gail You.
Hobby Sir.
Nixon (*shouting*) Right! Everybody, hands on heads, and fingers on lips.

Music. Black-out

ACT II

Christmas time at Whitewall's

The broom is stuck upside down in a US *desk. Trimmings, a star and a piece of crêpe paper adorn the broom, which is now a Christmas tree. Salty, Gail and Hobby take time putting up the tree*

Gail Christmas at Whitewall and love was in the air. All over the school there were Christmas trees and cards and trimmings, and every break time we would queue up to snog Martin Roebuck under some mistletoe in the reference section of the library.

Hobby Christmas also saw the culmination of Gail's interest in Mr Nixon.

Gail I love him . . .

Hobby You don't.

Gail I do . . . I am infatuated . . .

Hobby What's it feel like?

Gail Brilliant . . . I was on his table for Christmas dinner . . .

Hobby Yeh but does he love you?

Gail Dunno but I'll find out at the Christmas dance . . .

Hobby Why, what are you going to do?

Gail Snog him . . .

Hobby OOOOOOHHHH, you're not . . .

Gail I'll need some Dutch courage but I am . . .

Hobby I don't believe it . . .

Gail Listen, I've got it all worked out. We go to the off-licence, you go in and buy some cider.

Hobby Why me?

Gail Then I'll bring some spring onions from home. We'll drink the cider then eat the spring onions.

Hobby Spring onions, why?

Gail Because Doug and Mr Hatton will be on the door of the Christmas dance and Mrs Parry says if anyone is suspected of drinking alcohol they won't be allowed in . . . And I want to make sure I get in.

Hobby Are you sure Mr Nixon is going to the dance?

Gail Course he is, I've asked him a dozen times. I've sent him forty cards in the Christmas post.

Hobby Must have cost you a fortune?

Gail No my aunty works in a card shop, anyway it's the thought that counts.

Hobby So I went into the off-licence, and bought two large bottles of cider.

Gail Which we drank through a straw . . . And then we stuffed ourselves with spring onions.

Mr Hatton Bloody hell. Have you been eating spring onions?

Hobby That was Mr Hatton's reaction as we came into the disco ...

Gail Brilliant we're in, I told you it'd work, I'm slightly merry but not out of control.

Hobby I feel sick. I hate onions.

Gail Salty?

Salty What?

Gail Have you seen Mr Nixon?

Salty No, is he coming? Brilliant.

Gail Is he here yet?

Salty Hey can you smell onions?

Hobby Niko hadn't arrived, he was up in the pub with the rest of the staff, and he was sat very near to Miss Jackie Prime. Meanwhile down at the disco Mr Dean was doing Jimmy Saville impersonations and playing records that were three years out of date ...

Deanie Yes indeedy this is the sound of the Human League, "Don't you want me baby ..."

Gail Oh shit, look out, Oggy Moxon.

Salty becomes Oggy

Oggy Got you ...

Gail Hey oh ... great ...

Oggy Giz a kiss then ...

Gail Haven't you got any mistletoe?

Oggy I don't need mistletoe. Why didn't you come to my party, you owe me one ...

Gail Later, eh, maybe later ... I dashed away from Oggy leaving him wondering what perfume smells like onions ...

Hobby It is a fact of life that all teachers dance like retards. They dance like they're all out of a music documentary ... It must be the weight of all that knowledge in their heads which makes them look like they're in the back seat of an old Ford Cortina ... Mr Dean was a supreme example of bad dancing ...

Deanie Now then, now then what have we here? Uncle Ted, a bit of the old boogie woogie. (*He demonstrates extreme bad dancing*)

Hobby Oggy?

Salty becomes Oggy and kicks someone in the face. Hobby reacts

Hobby There'd been some trouble in the toilets, Oggy Moxon had hit Kev Jones for nothing ...

Gail Kev said that Oggy hit him because he fancied me ... Oggy tried to get me to dance but both times I left him and went to the toilets ... (*She moves to* US)

Nixon Simon Patterson, very smart ... Merry Christmas.

Hobby Merry Christmas, sir ...

Nixon Where's Salty?

Hobby I think he's dancing. Gail's in the loo ... Have you been drinking, sir?

Nixon Only a few pints, I'm in my new car.

Hobby Yeh you need a car when you're drinking and driving.

Nixon The Christmas dance had all the seriousness of a big disco, and the fifteen and sixteen years olds looked stunning done up to the nines, and only Mr Moorcroft, Head of RE seemed not to be moved by the gyrating bottoms and boobs ... At ten-thirty when things seemed like they were bubbling Deanie played the last record, a smoocher and Gail Saunders appeared in my arms and suddenly my face was confronted by the strong smell of onion ...

Salty, as Nixon and Gail smooch. Hobby, as Oggy Moxon, hangs around

Gail It was fantastic ...

Nixon It felt rather awkward, I didn't know how tight to hold Gail or where to put my hands ...

Parry Mrs Parry looked on, she felt a mixture of jealousy and condemnation. But it wasn't unknown for teachers to dance with students especially at Christmas. After all, as she had said, students were treated like young adults here at Whitewall.

Gail Doug the caretaker cleared the dance floor in a few minutes. And just as I was going to kiss Mr Nixon, he turned his head to wish Doug——

Nixon (*turning his head*) –a merry Christmas, Doug ...

Hobby Oggy Moxon had seen Gail and Niko dancing but he left the hall in silence ...

Gail Mr Nixon said that he would give me a lift down home, Salty and Hobby decided to walk it home and maybe get a kebab ...

Nixon I got into my car, an A reg Escort, and Gail jumped in beside me, and before I knew it, into the back jumped Oggy Moxon ...

Hobby becomes Oggy Moxon

Oggy Oh yeh, what's all this then? Bit of slap and tickle with the drama teacher, Gail. I thought all drama wallas were puffballs?

Nixon Will you get out, Oggy?

Oggy Will you get out, Oggy? No I will not.

Nixon Get out.

Oggy No, let's go a ride, eh ... ? Drop me down home, will you?

Nixon Get out.

Oggy Make me.

Nixon Get out ...

Oggy Make me ...

Nixon I shan't say it again ...

Oggy I shan't say it again. Come on, sir, make me get out ...

Nixon This is my car, I'm not in school hours, now get out ...

Gail Come on, Oggy ... It's not fair.

Oggy What's not fair? You want me to go so that you can have Mr Nixon all to yourself?

Nixon I'm going to get Mrs Parry ...

Oggy What the fuck is she going to do about it?

Nixon Will you get bloody out ...

Oggy You make me . . .
Nixon Arrgh . . .
Gail Oggy!!

Nixon hits Oggy in the face. Screaming. Oggy pulls himself out of the car

Oggy You've broke my nose, you bastard . . .
Gail Mr Nixon . . .
Oggy You bastard . . .
Hobby There was blood everywhere . . .
Gail I was screaming, Nixon was shaking.
Nixon A few members of staff came running from the school . . .
Hobby Oggy staggered away from the car. (*As Oggy*) Our Nobby'll get you
  Nixon . . . Wait till next term our Nobby'll hammer you. (*Pause*) And he
  was off into the dark. It was like a film . . . Everyone was shouting and
  trying to calm things . . . And in the distance you could hear Oggy Moxon
  shouting . . . "I'm gonna do you, Nixon. I'm gonna do you . . ."
Gail As we stood, a boy ran past us and jumped into his father's car . . . And
  a voice bellowed out . . .
Nixon Stop running, Simon Patterson!

Black-out. After a pause the Lights come up again

New Year. The Staff-room

Parry Morning, Jeff.
Nixon Morning, Mrs Parry.
Whitham Happy New Year.
Parry Happy New Year.
Whitham Had a nice time?
Nixon Lovely thanks, we went away . . . (*He starts to dismantle the
  Christmas tree*)
Parry So did we . . .
Whitham We stayed at home.
Parry You'll never guess what?
Whitham Go on.
Parry Jackie Prime got married, to Colin Short, Head of PE from Saint
  George's, did it over Christmas.
Whitham I didn't know. . . .
Parry Neither did I . . .
Nixon What was that?
Parry For Prime read Short . . . He's a hunk of a fella all man . . .
Nixon Oh . . . Happy New Year . . .
Parry You did what, Mr Nixon? Said Mrs Parry. Her yellow dress clashing
  with her pink blouse.
Nixon I . . . erm . . . erm . . . headbutted him in the face.
Parry If he decides to report this to the police or to his parents I'm afraid
  you're for the high jump.
Gail But Oggy Moxon didn't report the incident to either his dad or the
  police, but he told Nobby, and Nobby said that he would fix Nixon.

Nixon During every lesson I had one eye on the main entrance in case Oggy's brother appeared. And I wondered how many staff had said to how many kids, "Bring your dad up" and then wondered all day if they would.

Hobby Three or four days went by and nothing happened, Oggy's brother didn't appear and many teachers winked at Mr Nixon as much as to say "nice one".

Music

Nixon's bedsit

Nixon Most of my nights were spent indoors marking, going over the same mistakes and the same right answers. I was turning into a monk. I lived close to the school so I couldn't go to the local pub it was full of the sixth form, and I didn't know whether to be all mates or to tell the landlord that they were under age. So I stayed in and listened to Janis Ian and Dire Straits, and waited to see if I'd get an interview at Saint George's ...

The Main Hall

Gail During January the shine seemed to go off Nixon.

Salty And once we heard that he was applying somewhere else we sort of drifted away for a bit ... But we had a laugh. One day he asked us in drama to do a play about corporal punishment in schools, so we, Hobby, me and Gail did this thing about school killers.

Hobby Right, in the staff-room there's a red phone, like a batphone, and it glows really red when someone's on the other line.

Gail And in each classroom under the desk there's a buzzer, so if a teacher gets into some trouble or has a kid who is getting stroppy she can press the buzzer, and the phone rings.

Salty Right, in the staff-room, just like sat about all day drinking coffee, and reading ancient books are these ninjas, Japanese martial arts experts, who are trained to kill kids, with karate chops or sharp stars that they throw. And in the staff-room are a number of wires, so that these ninjas——

Hobby —when they get the call——

Salty —can jump out of the window of the staff-room and be at the root of the problem in a few seconds ...

Gail Right I'm the French assistant, and I'm teaching ...

Hobby I'm Rachael Steele—and I throw something at the board.

Gail (*with a French accent*) Who was that ... Who was that who was throwing missles towards my head? This is very dangerous and could be if someone gets hurt ... Was it you, Rachael?

Hobby What, miss?

Gail You know what?

Hobby No I don't, you frog ...

Gail And then suddenly the French assistant presses the buzzer for insolence.

Salty The phone rings ...

Hobby The ninjas are in action . . . Out of the staff-room window, coffee all over the place . . .

Gail Five seconds later . . . They arrive, kick the door down, tear gas all over the place . . .

Hobby The teacher had a mask secreted in her desk.

Gail Merci, ninja . . .

Salty Bonjour.

Gail The French assistant is back at work . . .

Hobby A call is made to Mr and Mrs Steele, would they like to come and collect the remains of their daughter Rachael from the school morgue. She was killed during a French lesson. Thank you . . .

Nixon It was stories like that, which kept I, Jeff Nixon, alive at Whitewall. And to my surprise the kids in drama got better and better, their imagination knew no bounds . . .

Gail You can't teach imagination, can you, sir?

Nixon I don't know . . .

Gail When was the battle of Hastings?

Nixon Ten sixty-six.

Gail What can you do with a brick?

Nixon Eh?

Gail What can you do with a brick? I saw this in a magazine . . .

Nixon Build a house . . .

Gail Yeh and . . . ?

Nixon Throw it.

Gail That shows the violent side of you. You can do unlimited things with a brick. You can drill a hole in it and wear it around your neck . . . You could marry a brick . . .

Hobby My cousin married a prick.

Gail There's lots of different answers. It says in this magazine that you can exercise your imagination, that's what we do in drama.

Hobby And art . . .

Gail Yeh but we don't do it in much else, do we? We're like robots. Who invaded England in ten sixty-six? Arm up, Norman the Conqueror. Arm down, computer programme complete.

Music

Mrs Parry's office

Nixon On January the twenty-first Mrs Parry called me to her office. She said it was urgent. Oggy has pressed charges, I knew it.

Parry Jeff. Thank God you're here.

Nixon What's the matter, is it Oggy Moxon?

Parry Worse.

Nixon His brother . . . Nobby . . . He's come to fix me?

Parry No. Can you do Koko? Mr Gill, who had the part slipped a disc last night building the set. Can you step into the breach, Jeff? I'd regard it as a great personal favour?

Nixon What about asking Mr Basford?

Parry Derek Basford is never a Koko, Jeff.

Nixon But I'm in the chorus.

Parry You can do that as well, do it for me, Jeff . . . You can't let me down, Jeff Nixon.

Nixon And so it was that Mrs Parry got me to play Koko.

Parry Wonderful, wonderful, we rehearse Wednesdays and Sunday . . . See you Sunday.

Gail When Mr Basford heard the news he went barmy with the cover rota.

Nixon And for the next three weeks, I was on cover all the time, French, German, physics, childcare, rural studies, needlework.

Music

The Mikado *rehearsals*

Parry Pick your teeth up, Mr Dean . . . Just pick them up and carry on singing . . . Move left, dear, move left . . . Good . . . There's no need to slouch in the chorus, Mr Basford. Remember you are gentlemen of Japan not lepers. Dignity.

Nixon Three members of the chorus were smoking.

Parry Carry on, carry on . . .

Nixon Mrs Parry's last production, *The Pirates*, lasted eight and a half hours . . . This looks like it could be longer . . .

Doug Face the front . . . Sing out front . . .

Parry Stay on stage, don't come out and watch, stay in the wings . . . It's no good saying "I was just coming to watch this bit", stay on stage . . .

Nixon The stage was a cattle market . . .

Parry Carry on, carry on, just do it . . .

Nixon But for Mrs Parry it was close enough for jazz.

Parry Amateurs, Mr Nixon, never work with animals, children and amateurs.

Nixon I'm sure it'll be . . . erm . . . great, Mrs Parry.

Parry I do hope so, Mr Nixon. This is my fifth *Mikado*, I haven't quite got it right yet . . . But we're trying. Do you know your lines yet?

Nixon Yes.

Parry Oh . . . Well, marvellous.

Nixon Would you like me to get up and do my bit?

Parry Oh no, if you know your lines you needn't bother coming till the dress rehearsal, I know you'll be brilliant . . . OK everyone, let's press on, where's the Mikado, where's Poo-bah, where's Nanky Poo?

Doug They're in the music room playing bridge.

Parry Well tell them that I need them NOW!

Doug Oi . . . you're bloody on . . .

Nixon During February the mock exams were held in the main hall.

Doug Doug, the caretaker was as smug as a Cheshire cat. Haha you'll not be able to do any drama now, Niko . . . Basford's scotched you this time. Seven weeks these desks have got to stay in here . . . He could have put these in the gym but Dave Fisher asked him not to . . .

Nixon It's OK, Doug, I'm going to do all my drama classes in the back room of the *George and Dragon*.

Doug I hope you get that job at Saint George's ... Let them have a basin full of you ...

Nixon I reckon that I could teach drama anywhere and no-one would mind. In the cookery class.

The class scream. They are improvising around the Marat-Sade. *Gail tells the audience she is Jean-Paul Marat*

Hobby In the coal bunker ...

Salty In the boiler house ...

Gail Canteen ...

Hobby Sports hall showers ...

Salty School gates ...

Gail Swimming baths ...

Hobby Woolworth's ...

Salty Simon Patterson's bedroom.

All Stop running, Simon Patterson.

Nixon What I couldn't fathom is why a school didn't have a space that was solely used for exams. You would have thought that somewhere along the way from the first paper ever sat at Oxford that some boffin would have seen that schools need purpose-built rooms to do exams in. But then what did I know?

Parry You knew that you'd got an interview at Saint George's ... Congratulations, said Mrs Parry.

Nixon She was one of my referees. So joining the G and S had its advantages. But rumour had it that Basford wrote all references and I knew he'd be happy to see me go. Drama didn't feature in his scheme of things.

Hobby becomes Mr Basford

Basford Mr Nixon, can I ask you to keep the noise down? I've got a sixth form group in the lecture theatre, we can't hear ourselves, think.

Nixon You what, Mr Basford?

Basford It's like an asylum in here.

Nixon Yeh great, isn't it? They've really taken to it. We're doing the *Marat-Sade*. It's set in a bath house.

Basford Quiet. Keep them quiet. I said keep the noise down.

Nixon Hang on, Mr Basford, I wouldn't do that to you.

Basford It's like a flaming riot.

Nixon They're enjoying themselves.

Basford Enjoying themselves? They sound like they're screaming to get out of your lesson, they can't stand it.

Nixon I'm sure that there's more sixth formers screaming to get out of yours ...

Basford Watch your step, Nixon.

Nixon He was pissed off because I'd got an interview. Apparently, according to Mr Dean, he had applied for the Head at Saint George's job and had not had his references taken up ... It had made him a bitter man ...

Music

Saint George's Private School

Ms Coates Well thank you very much, Mr Nixon, it's been a pleasure talking to you. Obviously we have other candidates to see but we should be able to let you know either way before the end of spring term.

Mrs Clifton His interview at Saint George's had gone very well. Mrs Clifton, one of the governors of Saint George's thought he would be outstanding. She also thought he would be a marvellous asset to Saint George's Amateur Players, a society run by Mrs Clifton.

Nixon Saint George's was a sanctuary compared with Whitewall, kids stood up when a teacher went into a class, no-one leaped for the door when the bell rang, and their drama studio was pure heaven, I was told that the caretaker at Saint George's often sat in and watched drama classes, and not a single person had walked through the drama studio ever.

Hobby Chalk and cheese.

Nixon That's the difference. Unbelievable.

Gail Colditz Jeff. The great escape.

A choir sings

Tennis courts

Gail One Wednesday when not a lot was happening Mr Basford had organized a tennis competition. Some of the third year were allowed out on to the courts.

Salty You mean *court*.

Gail Whitewall only had one decent court. The rest were like dirt tracks.

Salty Mr Nixon had been invited to take part at the last minute because Mick Edwards had a meeting with the Social Services.

Hobby Forty love, game Basford. Hard luck, Mr Dean.

Gail Mr Dean got thrashed and so he took his class back to the mobiles to study the unification of Germany, he was a bad loser.

Hobby Forty love, game Basford. Bad luck, Mr Fisher, you've got bowlegs. Couldn't stop a pig in a ginnel . . .

Gail Mr Basford was an ace tennis player, Jackie Prime told me that he was a county player in his youth.

Salty He had no kit, he looked like Barry Wobschall. Borrowed a pair of pumps from big Pete Saxon and Salty lent him some shorts . . . Somehow, mysteriously, got a bye into the final. And in the final played Mr Basford, who had annihilated Jackie Prime's husband. He was glad about that.

Hobby Bad luck, Mr Short.

Salty Hey Shorty, too much bed, not enough sleep. When Nixon came on to the court all the kids were laughing.

They laugh

Gail Niko looked like somebody from Doctor Barnardo's. Nothing fitted him.

Hobby Are you sure you know what you're doing, Mr Nixon?

Nixon All the kids had their faces pushed against the wire of the courts.

They pull a face, to show this

Gail Go on, Mr Basford, smash the ball through his head. That was Oggy Moxon.

Hobby Forty love.

Gail Smash him, Basford.

Hobby Game Basford.

Gail Jackie Prime was smirking the sort of smirk that only PE staff can do.

Hobby Game Basford ...

They play tennis by tapping a chair and watching a ball

Gail Come on, Mr Basford, humiliate him ... Shouted Oggy, like a wild animal ...

Salty And he tried to ... It was like watching Christians in the Coliseum ...

Hobby Love all.

Salty Fifteen love ...

Hobby Well done, Mr Nixon. You've won a point. I didn't know you could play.

Nixon Yeh, what he didn't know, what none of the staff knew was that I was an under-nineteen tennis international ... And I thrashed Basford. One six, six love, six love.

Gail Mr Basford left the courts in haste. All the kids looked gob-smacked.

Nixon I could have spared him, but why should I ... ? As I walked from the courts I bumped into Oggy Moxon ...

Gail becomes Oggy Moxon

Oggy Our Nobby's gonna fix you.

Nixon Great.

Oggy Hey ... I thought you were a fart ... Didn't know you could play tennis.

Nixon Neither did Mr Basford. And you tell your Nobby if he comes up here, I'll shove this down his neck.

Oggy Right ... I'll tell him ...

Music

Hobby With the end of term only six weeks off Niko had this idea of me, Gail and Salty doing a play about school-life for the leavers.

Salty It was great because Niko had arranged for us to get out of other lessons, 'cos we didn't have exams.

Gail And most teachers were happy to let us go ...

Salty It was brilliant, like we had the freedom of the city ... It's great ... I'm missing maths to do drama, brilliant ...

Gail Salty was over the moon. He was running around school like a head-less chicken. He had written in spray paint on the side of the gym——

Salty —Mr Basford is a fat Basford.

Hobby All the staff thought it was fairly amusing. Basford didn't, he put Salty on a long list of Easter leavers who had to see Mrs Parry ...

Parry You don't come to school to fool about, Ian, to waste your time. We treat you like young adults and we expect you to behave accordingly. I don't think that writing swear words on a wall is a mature thing to do. Do you?

Salty No, Mrs Parry.

Parry Well why did you do it, Ian?

Salty Fed up, Mrs Parry.

Parry Fed up of what? What are you fed up of, Ian?

Salty Loads of things, Mrs Parry. Having to leave school.

Parry Well we all have to leave school sometime, don't we?

Salty Yeh but that's it, Mrs Parry, out there, there's nothing, it's just a load of lies. A load of promises that never happen. I'm sixteen, and I might have wasted my time in school and I've got to bugger off. Maybe I'm not ready for that . . . I've woken up too late, Mrs Parry. I don't want to be a piece of rhubarb . . . I want another chance . . . What's the word I am? I'm a late developer, Mrs Parry, I've got some interest, I've found something I'm interested in—with Mr Nixon. Who is it that says we only have one chance, Mrs Parry? Is it God, 'cos if it is it's not the same God my mother talks about . . .

Parry Everyone has to grow up, Ian. Leaving school is just a part of growing up.

Salty Yeh but nobody out there cares. If people did care you'd be able to say to me, "All right, Salty, stop on, start again, have another crack" . . . I can't negotiate, Mrs Parry, you can't negotiate . . . Who is it who traps us both? Politicians . . . them men on the telly with funny haircuts, them men who talk about choice and equality and fairness . . . Why don't any of them live on our estate? Why don't I see any of them down the welfare hall or at the Bingo? . . . They're not bothered about us . . . Do you believe what they say, Mrs Parry? It's all a load of lies. They don't care, and what's worse, you know, is that they're not bothered that they don't care. Then I turned and left her room.

Parry Ian Salt, come here immediately . . .

Music

The Staff-room

Whitham Congratulations. You did it.

Jones Well done, Jeff.

Whitham When do you start?

Nixon September.

Jones Another success for the escape committee.

Whitham We'll have a drink after *The Mikado*, said Maureen Whitham, who was playing Sing Sing. I've got my job in local radio, make it a double celebration.

Nixon I was obviously very pleased. The kids said that I would change, going to a snob school. But it was an unbelievable feeling. And for some reason Jackie Short, née Prime kissed me . . . I felt like a great weight had been lifted from my shoulders, I could breath once more, I was free . . . Thank God I was free . . .

Jones Hey, I've got another interview, it's my seventeenth this month.
Whitham Orrrrr ...
Nixon The opening night of *The Mikado* was extra-or-dinary.

Black-out. After a pause, the Lights come up again

Parry Thank you, thank you.

Gail presents her with a bouquet

Thank you, thank you all. I'd like if I may to thank everyone concerned. I'd like to thank Gerald my husband for being so patient, and also Daphne and Clarence my two wonderful children, and of course Doug the caretaker, without whom this production would not have been possible. And also all the backstage team ... Come on, fellas, let's have you out here ...
Nixon It was the shortest production of *The Mikado* in history, fifty-five minutes. Forty-six pages of the libretto had been skipped over. But it was still a success.
Parry And I'd like to thank, Simon and Peter for numbering the chairs.
Nixon The thank yous went on for an hour.
Parry And Joyce, Hilda and Francis who did the little buns and cakes, and how lovely they were as well.
Nixon The cast stood there wilting.
Parry And Martin and Chris for cutting the squares of cinemoid which made all those lovely colours. And to Desmond and Sue who helped park the cars. Thanks to you all.
Gail On the last night of *The Mikado* Mrs Parry threw a party in the sixth-form common room. Everyone chatted and drank Pomagne from paper cups. Basford was there. (*As Basford*) So, I suppose it's congratulations, Mr Nixon?
Nixon Sorry?
Basford Congratulations. You must feel very pleased with yourself?
Nixon Not really.
Basford You were a very good Koko, it was quite a swan-song.
Nixon Thanks very much, Derek.
Basford I'm sure you'll have a great time over at Saint George's. It's what you want, isn't it? They're quite into drama over there. The twins are thinking of drama as an option. This is not a school for drama, never has been, never will be.
Nixon I'll miss the kids.
Basford Not for long. You just have a thought for us, still stuck here. Mind you, every cloud has a silver lining as they say, Mrs Parry has just asked me if I'd like to play Nathan Detroit in next term's *Guys and Dolls*.
Nixon And are you?
Basford My dear boy, the part was made for me.
Hobby All the kids were really sad when Nixon left, and me and Salty and Gail all cried.
Gail We never saw Niko again. Somebody told us that he was having a good time at Saint George's, and that all the posh kids loved him. When

we left school I got a job typing, and I did some dance. I was also in the chorus of *Guys and Dolls.*

Hobby And I'd got this job with my uncle. And Oggy Moxon ... it was like on a farm, hard work, but good fun.

Salty I didn't know what I did. I could think anything up. I wanted to write songs for Wham and be a millionaire, but Mr Harrison said it was too far-fetched ... But I'd like to ...

A school bell rings. End of school. The Lights change. Salty, Gail and Hobby are lost. They move around the stage slowly, and pick up their bags. Silence

Gail Oh well ... that's it then.

Hobby The end.

Salty Mr Harrison, can I just say before we go, sir, don't leave, sir. The kids here need teachers like you. Don't go to that snob school, sir.

Gail Sir, if you stay, we'll come back and bug you. We'll let you know how we're getting on. I'll come and cut your hair if you like ... I'm doing a scheme at the hairdresser's, it's twenty-five quid but my mam says it's better than nothing. Just.

Salty Sir, I'm doing a scheme, painting and decorating, should be a laugh, I'm crap at art. Might end up on an advert ... Be a star then, sir ...

Gail Don't leave, sir ...

Hobby I'm doing french polishing, gonna hate it.

Salty If you stay and do another drama play, we'll be in it ...

Hobby Best thing I've ever done at school this ... It's the only thing I'll remember ...

Salty We could have a laugh, start a group up.

Gail And rehearse at nights ...

Salty Hey we could do all sorts ... *Marat-Sade.*

Gail Comedies.

Hobby Tragedies.

Gail Westerns.

Salty Kung fu ...

Gail Sir, romances ...

Hobby Sex plays ...

Salty Sir ... I've got it ... Why don't you do *The Mikado* ... ?

Gail *Mikado.* Sir, you said that was shit.

Hobby Anyway ... See you, sir ... See you, Mrs Hudson ...

Salty Yeh. Thanks, sir ...

Gail Yeh.

Hobby Yeh thanks.

Salty Yeh.

Gail Thanks a lot.

Salty See you ...

Hobby Tara ...

Gail Yeh.

They walk away. They freeze. "Gentleman of Japan" from The Mikado *plays*

Black-out

FURNITURE AND PROPERTY LIST

ACT I

On stage: 2 double desks. *On them:* 3 plastic briefcases, files, newspapers and
magazines
Old locker
Broom
3 chairs
2 single desks
3 bags
Satchel
Plastic bags
Sports bags

Off stage: Funny nose and glasses **(Gail)**

Personal: **Gail:** piece of paper in pocket

ACT II

Set: Broom upside down as Christmas tree with trimmings, star, crêpe paper

Off stage: Bouquet **(Stage Management)**

LIGHTING PLOT

Practical fittings required: nil

Interior. The same scene throughout

ACT I

To open: General interior lighting

Cue 1	**Salty:** "And it's called *Teechers.*" *Increase lighting*	(Page 3)
Cue 2	Music *Black-out*	(Page 19)

ACT II

To open: General interior lighting

Cue 3	**Nixon:** "Stop running, Simon Patterson!" *Black-out. Revert to original lighting for next scene*	(Page 23)
Cue 4	**Nixon** ". . . *The Mikado* was extra-or-dinary." *Black-out. Revert to original lighting for next scene*	(Page 31)
Cue 5	School bell *The lights change*	(Page 32)
Cue 6	*The Mikado* plays *Black-out*	(Page 32)

EFFECTS PLOT

Please read the notice on page 36 concerning the use of copyright music and commercial recordings

ACT I

To open: Music. Cut when ready

Cue 1	**Salty:** "And it's called *Teechers*." *A sudden burst of music*	(Page 3)
Cue 2	**Parry:** ". . . and not for anyone else." *Music. Fade after a few moments*	(Page 3)
Cue 3	**Hobby:** ". . . he's new." *School bell rings*	(Page 6)
Cue 4	**Hobby** and **Gail:** "E.T., phone home . . ." *Music. Fade after a few moments*	(Page 9)
Cue 5	**Nixon:** ". . . at break-time. Silly sods." *Music. Fade after a few moments*	(Page 11)
Cue 6	**Gail:** "And lock up your daughters . . ." *Music. Fade after a few moments*	(Page 12)
Cue 7	**Gail:** "A choir was singing." *A choir sings*	(Page 14)
Cue 8	**Nixon:** ". . . could not be said of Whitewall." *The choir stops*	(Page 14)
Cue 9	**Gail** exits *Music. Fade after a few moments*	(Page 15)
Cue 10	**Doug** moves to US *Music. Fade after a few moments*	(Page 16)
Cue 11	**Nixon:** ". . . and fingers on lips." *Music*	(Page 19)

ACT II

Cue 12	**Hobby:** ". . . as we came into the disco . . ." *Music for disco scene as required*	(Page 21)
Cue 13	**Hobby:** ". . . as to say 'nice one'." *Music. Fade after a few moments*	(Page 24)
Cue 14	**Gail:** ". . . computer programme complete." *Music. Fade after a few moments*	(Page 25)

MUSIC USE NOTE

Licensees are solely responsible for obtaining formal written permission from copyright owners to use copyrighted music in the performance of this play and are strongly cautioned to do so. If no such permission is obtained by the licensee, then the licensee must use only original music that the licensee owns and controls. Licensees are solely responsible and liable for all music clearances and shall indemnify the copyright owners of the play(s) and their licensing agent, Samuel French, against any costs, expenses, losses and liabilities arising from the use of music by licensees. Please contact the appropriate music licensing authority in your territory for the rights to any incidental music.

IMPORTANT BILLING AND CREDIT REQUIREMENTS

If you have obtained performance rights to this title, please refer to your licensing agreement for important billing and credit requirements.